The Collab[...]

Anthony Mc[...]

methuen | drama

LONDON · NEW YORK · OXFORD · NEW DELHI · SYDNEY

METHUEN DRAMA
Bloomsbury Publishing Plc
50 Bedford Square, London, WC1B 3DP, UK
1385 Broadway, New York, NY 10018, USA
29 Earlsfort Terrace, Dublin 2, Ireland

BLOOMSBURY, METHUEN DRAMA and the Methuen
Drama logo are trademarks of Bloomsbury Publishing Plc

First published in Great Britain 2022

Cover concept and design by Emilie Chen.
Photography by Jenny Anderson.

A catalogue record for this book is available from the British Library.

Library of Congress Control Number: 2022932019

ISBN: PB: 978-1-3503-3296-6
ePDF: 978-1-3503-3297-3
eBook: 978-1-3503-3298-0

Series: Modern Plays

Typeset by Mark Heslington Ltd, Scarborough, North Yorkshire
Printed and bound in Great Britain

To find out more about our authors and books visit
www.bloomsbury.com and sign up for our newsletters.

Young Vic

A Young Vic production, first performed at the Young Vic

The Collaboration

A new play by Anthony McCarten

THE COLLABORATION

By Anthony McCarten

The Collaboration had its world premiere at the Young Vic on 16 February 2022.

CAST *(in alphabetical order)*

Maya	**Sofia Barclay**
Andy Warhol	**Paul Bettany**
Bruno Bischofberger	**Alec Newman**
Jean-Michel Basquiat	**Jeremy Pope**

CREATIVE TEAM

Director	**Kwame Kwei-Armah**
Set and Costume Designer	**Anna Fleischle**
Lighting Designer	**Mark Henderson**
Sound Designer	**Emma Laxton**
Projection Designer	**Duncan McLean**
Casting Director	**Isabella Odoffin CDG**
Composer	**Ayanna Witter-Johnson**
DJ/VJ	**Xana**
Assistant Director and Production Dramaturg	**Olivia Nwabali**
Assistant Set and Costume Designer	**Tina Torbey**

Produced in partnership with Eleanor Lloyd, Anthology Theatre, Stanley Buchthal and Eilene Davidson in association with Denis O'Sullivan.

With thanks to Rupert Goold and the Almeida Theatre for their early support of this play.

Cover Artwork: Art direction by Emilie Chen. Photography by Jenny Anderson.

Young Vic

About the Young Vic

For fifty years, the Young Vic has produced new plays, classics, musicals, adaptations of books, short films, digital projects and game-changing forms of theatre, attracting large audiences from many different backgrounds.

They forge deep connections in their neighbourhood through their ambitious Taking Part programme, where they engage with over 15,000 people every year via a wide range of projects, helping their community to develop their creative skills, build meaningful relationships, and tell compelling stories about the world we live in. The Young Vic give 10% of their tickets free to those who experience the biggest barriers accessing the arts, irrespective of box office demand, and they are committed to keeping their ticket prices low.

The Young Vic Creators Program, the only scheme of its kind, has been running for nearly twenty years and offers theatre makers unique opportunities to develop their craft through skills workshops, peer-led projects, paid assistant directing roles through the Genesis Fellow, the Jerwood Assistant Director Program and the Boris Karloff Trainee Assistant Director Program, as well as access to the Genesis Directors Network. Twice a year, the recipient of the Genesis Future Directors Award directs a show in The Clare theatre at the Young Vic with full support from the Young Vic's creative, administrative and production teams, enabling the theatre to support and nurture an emerging director as a part of the Young Vic programme.

For many years, the Young Vic has been synonymous with inclusivity, accessibility and creativity. They catalyse debate and channel their work into the digital world, to reach new audiences and continue conversations outside of their four walls. The Young Vic foster emerging talent and collaborate with some of the world's finest directors, performers and creatives; creating award-winning productions which engage with the world we live in.

Artistic Director: **Kwame Kwei-Armah**

Interim Executive Director: **Sarah Nicholson**

youngvic.org

Public Support

Season Support

The Young Vic's 2022 season is also supported by the Genesis Foundation and IHS Markit.

We gratefully acknowledge Ian Burford and Alec Cannell for generously supporting the Young Vic's mission.

Anthony McCarten is a New Zealand-born playwright, novelist, journalist, television writer and filmmaker. He is best known for writing the biopics *The Theory of Everything* (2014), *Darkest Hour* (2017), *Bohemian Rhapsody* (2018) and *The Two Popes* (2019). A double BAFTA-winning screenwriter, he has been nominated four times for Academy Awards, among them nominations for Best Adapted Screenplay for *The Theory of Everything* and *The Two Popes*. He is the author of ten previous plays and writer of the 'book' for the upcoming Neil Diamond Broadway musical, *A Beautiful Noise* (2022). *The Collaboration* is the second instalment of his *The Worship Trilogy*, the other two parts being *The Two Popes* and *Wednesday at Warren's, Friday at Bill's*. As a sequence, they separately explore our worship of religion, art and money. He lives in London.

The Collaboration

PART of THE WORSHIP TRILOGY:

*The Two Popes, The Collaboration,
Wednesday at Warren's Friday at Bill's*

Cast

Andy Warhol
Jean-Michel Basquiat
Bruno Bischofberger
Maya

Act One

Prologue

The sound of Miles Davis' 'Lonely Fire' rises.

Lights up on:

Scene One

Bruno Bischofberger's Gallery, NY

Andy Warhol (*56*), *wearing his iconic white wig, faces the audience, inspecting an array of paintings that the audience will have to imagine – a wall of twenty-four Basquiat works arranged four paintings high and six across.* **Andy**, *staring into space, is variously fascinated, shocked, amazed, excited and jealous.*

Andy   Oh my God.

Moving, inspecting further.

Andy   It's too much.

Inspecting further.

Andy   No, really.

Andy *is joined by Swiss art dealer,* **Bruno Bischofberger** (*45*) *so that now both men stare out into the auditorium in wonder . . .*

Bruno   Well?

Andy   Oh my God Bruno, why did you bring me here?

Bruno   You don't like it? Andy? What do you think? Genius, no? For sure. So you can see what all the fuss is about. What do you think? Really? Tell me. He's mine now. I represent him now.

Andy   I know you do. I'm furious with you. You're such a traitor, Bruno. I thought the Swiss were supposed to be dependable. But you're always moving on to the hot new thing, forgetting everybody who made you rich. You're worse than a cheap drag queen. Hot isn't always best you know. Leaving me behind. You know I made you a lot of money. At least I think I did. Didn't I?

Bruno   A lot, sure. And we're only just beginning. We lost a little steam lately, sure, but we're coming back.

Inspecting further.

Andy   I don't know. They're so . . . *busy*. You know? There's so much going on. Is it too much? Or am I getting old? And so much *anger*. Look at these . . . I mean look at all these *skulls* and gravestones. I thought *I* was bleak. But they're so great.

Beat.

How does he get so much . . . *energy*? I'm exhausted just looking at them. And look at all these words and symbols everywhere! What do they all mean? Do you know?

Bruno *shrugs.*

Andy   Bruno? (*Pause.*) What's he trying to say? (*Pause.*) And why do they have to be so ugly? Did he tell you? Does he talk about that? They're so ugly and angry and kinda violent. He's really in trouble I think. Don't you think so, Bruno?

Beat.

I've seen this before. I think he must really be in trouble.

Beat.

I remember the first time I saw him. He was sleeping in the doorway of my place on Great Jones Street. I told my assistant to keep him out of the building. I was so afraid of him. He was using drugs, and filthy, and you know how I am about germs. Seeing these painting, gee . . . I'm more afraid of him than ever.

Beat.

How long does it take Jean to do one of these things?

Bruno   A couple of hours. It's incredible.

Andy   A couple of hours? Oh my God. That's terrible.

Bruno   Why?

Andy   Why? Because that means he's faster than me! I'm so jealous! (*Sighs.*) Okay how much is he selling for? You have to tell me. Not more than me I hope.

Bruno   No. Not yet.

Andy *snaps him a competitive look.*

Bruno   Between fifty thousand and sixty thousand a piece, only . . . but climbing fast.

Andy   *I* don't get that anymore. That's kinda shocking. I mean . . .

Bruno   You need to give us something new Andy. I keep telling you.

Andy   But everything I do is different. What are you talking about, Bruno? You're meant to encourage me.

Bruno   I mean all the brand names, the icons, reinterpreting things we see or use everyday. Everything silk-screened. As great as they are, they're *expected* from you now. Forgive me, but when was the last time you picked up a brush and actually painted?

Andy   Oh.

Bruno   A pen and drew? Ten years? Twenty years?

Andy   People are so demanding! I'm human, even if I don't look it.

Bruno   The market's into paintings now.

Beat.

I think he's very great.

Andy (*somewhat shocked*)   You think he's great?

Bruno   I invited him to my home in Zurich. And I proposed something very exciting, involving you, that Jean-Michel has agreed to, absolutely, sure, no question, he wants it.

Andy   Wants what?

Bruno   A collaboration. With you.

Andy   With me? What do you mean 'a collaboration'?

Bruno   He wants to collaborate with you on a series of paintings, for sure. He's super excited. Admires you. Says you've been a great inspiration. And it might be good for you too Andy. I think so. You know you can learn a lot from the young. It's not only one way.

Andy   I don't know. Gee. Now I'm confused. Bruno, don't do this to me. I won't be able to sleep for a week now. I've never collaborated. What is a collaboration anyway?

Bruno   You add a touch, he adds a touch, and so on.

Andy   You mean, *paint* together, with *brushes?*

Bruno   You take turns. A *collaboration.*

Andy   Oh, no, Bruno . . . no . . .

Bruno   And then when we have enough works we have an incredible show, here, or at Gagosian . . .

Andy   . . . no, no . . .

Bruno   . . . or Mary Boone or Tony Shafrazi's, and it will be the greatest exhibition ever in the history of art.

Andy   Please don't exaggerate.

Bruno   Warhol versus Basquiat.

Andy   Versus? Gee, you make it sound so macho, like *a contest*. I don't know. I thought you said it would be a collaboration?

Bruno Sure, a collaboration, but . . . for the title of the greatest painter alive in the world today. Boxers are like painters, both smear their blood on the canvas.

Andy You're a poet, Bruno.

Bruno A collaboration . . . between rivals . . . to decide . . . who is the champ.

Andy *mulls this.*

Andy I'm not sure I'm up to that.

Bruno You look wonderful by the way. Super great.

Andy *touches the right side of his stomach.*

Andy No. I've never been the same since she shot me. Crazy bitch. No wonder I don't let people get close to me. They shoot you. With a gun. Isn't that unbelievable? What kind of a world are we living in? That's not how friends should behave. So rude.

Bruno Andy, come on. This will be great for you. You're the greatest painter in the world, there's absolutely no question. And everyone loves you, the world over –

Andy Stop saying that. It's really not true. My reputation is in tatters, museums won't take my works anymore, my prices are falling, they say I've ruined art for everybody. *Nobody* loves me, Bruno, and it's rotten of you to get my hopes up.

Bruno Of course they love you. You are adored, the problem with you Andy, is . . .

Andy What is the problem with me? Tell me.

Bruno *You don't know how to return love.*

Andy Gee. Do you think so? I think you're right. Oh my God. That explains *everything*. Thank you, Bruno.

Bruno You're welcome. So . . . what do I tell Jean? Shall I tell him you've said yes? Yes? Or no, Andy?

Andy, *getting a new idea, starts to warm to the offer . . .*

Andy   Will he let me film him?

Bruno   Film him?

Andy   Uh huh.

Bruno (*doubtful*)   Ooof, Andy, I don't know.

Andy *turns, starts to exit, stops, takes a flash photo of* **Jean**'s *art, then exits.*

Enter **Jean-Michel Basquiat** (*24*), *his hair a fountain of dreadlocks from the top of his head, the sides of his head shorn close. He's brooding, taciturn, not very talkative.*

Jean   I've changed my mind.

Bruno *re-enters.*

Bruno   Why? No! Why?

Jean *shrugs, walks around, looking at his paintings.*

Jean   You got me, you got me drunk. All that cheap Swiss wine.

Bruno   *French* wine. *Romanée-Conti*. You just drank it like it was cheap! (*Off* **Jean**'s *offended look.*) Say something. Jean?

Jean   No.

Bruno   No?

Jean   Call it off.

Bruno   I can't. It's all arranged. And Andy is super excited. You can't do this to him. You should have seen him. He came here, took one look at these works, and said 'I have to work with Jean.'

A spark of interest in **Jean** *but then –*

Jean   I don't collaborate anymore. I did some with Michael, and with Al, on the street, not anymore.

Bruno   'Bruno, make this happen,' he said, standing right here. You should have heard him: 'Oh gee, I *have* to do some paintings with this guy, he's a genius.'

Jean   He's old hat. (*Pause.*) Does anyone really care about Warhol now? All that fag silk screen stuff? Marilyns, Elvises, soup cans?

Bruno   This could be so incredible for you Jean. Your name linked, as equals, with the most famous living painter in the world.

Jean   Is he living?

Bruno   Stop it, Jean. He's in perfect health, that's very mean.

Jean   And who says I want to be 'equal' to Andy? I'm better than Andy already. I don't need this.

Bruno   Jean. This simply *has* to happen. It's all arranged. Two modern giants, coming together – it's like, like Picasso and Edvard Munch! Okay, Duchamp and Pollock . . . Dr Seuss and Sid Wicious I don't care! – It will launch you into the stratosphere, okay. You guys haven't painted a single painting yet but inside my chest I already hear the universal cry: 'I want it! I want it! I want it!'

Jean (*unimpressed*)   His whole dumb thing is about questioning what art is, you know. That's lame. And how come he doesn't paint anymore, you know? Just mechanically reproduces all these prints? There's no soul. I'm Dizzy Gillespie, blowing a riff, he's one of those pianos that plays all by itself. The same tune. Over and over. You seen those things? *Pink, pink plonk, pinkety pinkety pink.*

Bruno   He stopped painting because he doesn't believe in it. He stopped believing in painting twenty years ago. Decided the future was in film and photography, the moving image, mass reproduction.

Jean   Giant Brillo boxes? You serious?

Bruno   Sure. But he's searching for something new now. Looking for a new direction, I can feel it. He can learn from you. You could free him up. You could help a great artist.

Jean (*examining one painting*)   This one, I don't like this one anymore. Don't sell it.

Jean *takes this painting down, leans it against the wall, then walks to another painting.*

Bruno   No, but I, I, I love –

Jean   You just want to make money, Bruno – more and more and more and more and more money. Is that all art is about now?

Bruno   I also make money *for you*. You no longer sleep in doorways, Jean. They tell me you keep a permanent room at the Ritz now, just for when you feel like dropping in.

Bruno *puts the leaning painting back up on the wall.*

Bruno   I've helped . . . make that possible. And we're just beginning, you and me. So you have to trust Bruno now. This is a super-cool project that will have art lovers lined up from the gallery door to fucking JFK, I'm telling you, man.

Jean   Bankers.

Bruno   Art lovers, Jean. Like you. People who love art as much as you do.

Jean   I don't love art.

Jean *sits on the floor.*

Bruno   For someone who doesn't love art you make a fucking lot of it. Why make art then? Why, Jean?

Jean   I can't make shoes.

Bruno   'I can't make shoes.'

Jean   I make art coz I can't make shoes. Or taco chips. Or saxophones. Or automobiles. Or refrigerators. I'd much rather make refrigerators. How do you make a refrigerator? We should go into the refrigerator business.

Bruno   Just meet him, put a toe in the water, if you still think it won't work, if you're too far apart as artists, then . . . then we talk again. But please, Jean, I beg you. Begin the conversation.

Jean   I don't have anything to say to him. We speak different languages.

Beat.

I could, I could do it, but I don't want to. It's not my thing. I'm not here to bring Andy back from the dead.

Bruno *sags, gives up.*

Bruno   I'm sorry . . . I've tried. If you don't want to do it you don't want to do it. But it's a tragedy. It's a disaster.

Jean (*he draws words*)   Hurricanes are disasters . . . Mountains collapsing on villages . . . Asbestos is a disaster . . . A train hitting a school bus is a disaster.

Bruno   I will never get over this. But if you say No, what can I do?

Jean   You're giving up?

Bruno   It's what you want. I do what you want. Back to Zurich I go, my tail between my legs. And don't draw on my fucking floor.

Jean   Tell me what he *really* thinks of me.

Bruno   Andy?

Jean   What does he really think of me?

Bruno   I think . . . I think . . .

Beat.

. . . he's afraid of you. A little bit.

Jean   Why's Andy afraid of me?

Bruno   He's afraid . . . that you're overtaking him . . .
painting and painting like you do, while he just goes to
parties . . . your prices going up, his going down, that
frightens him. And he's getting old and he got shot and he's
afraid of germs and he still gets acne, at his age. Why
shouldn't he be afraid?

Jean (*gently yet firmly*)   Why's he afraid of me, Bruno?

Jean *steps right up to* **Bruno**, *making* **Bruno** *nervous.*

Bruno   He thinks . . . you're a threat to his entire
understanding of art.

Music up.

As **Jean** *stares at a painting, with a small smile forming on his lips*
. . .

. . . *a dancing* **Maya** *enters (***Jean**'s *27-year-old girlfriend), and we
transition to a dreamy sequence where* **Jean** *and* **Maya** *dance
together, vibe off each other, in tune with each other, two joyful souls
in the heyday of their love* . . .

As **Maya** *exits,* **Jean** *pulls on headphones and the music shrinks to
– the suggestion of what we might overhear coming from his
headphones* . . .

Scene Two

Andy Warhol's Studio, 860 Broadway, Union Square, NY

*White, very clean – sterile almost. On the walls, his Marilyns, his
Elvises, his Campbell's soup cans.*

Jean *looks over* **Andy**'s *art on the walls, then goes to face the
auditorium (the fourth wall) to continue his examination.*

Enter **Andy**. *He clocks* **Jean**'s *interest in his art.*

As **Jean** *turns, sees* **Andy**, *he takes from his shoulder bag a cassette
tape . . . Miles Davis.*

Jean   I brought over some music. I thought we . . . Do you like Miles? Andy?

Andy   Huh?

Jean   Miles Davis? I got a great jazz tape. I like to paint to jazz. Be-Bop. Is that . . .?

Andy   Oh. Jazz? Oh gee.

Jean   You don't like it?

Andy   Well. It's okay. But jazz, it goes on so *loooong*.

Jean   Miles Davis? You don't like Miles Davis? Come on! Then I don't think we can work together, you know. I'm serious.

The pattern is established, with both men testing each other, trading small jabs, slipping the other's punches.

Andy   You don't? Gee. That was quick. I better run after Bruno. He's going to be *so* disappointed.

Jean   Come on, man. It's Miles, man. How can you not like Miles?

Andy   My favourite story about Miles is . . . my *favourite* story . . . is when he told me about John Coltrane, complaining to him that he didn't know how to end his super-long solos and Miles advised, 'Try taking the fucking horn out of your mouth.'

Andy *laughs.* **Jean** *does not, suspecting one-upmanship here.*

Andy   Isn't that grrreat? You gotta love him for that. Any artist with wit should be paid attention to. All gloomy bastards should be clubbed to death.

Jean   Does that include me, Andy?

Andy   I've issued a stay of execution for you until we're done. But from what I've seen you could lighten up a bit.

Jean *returns to looking at* **Andy***'s art on the walls . . .*

Andy   All these screaming black figures you paint . . . how many screaming negroes can you do? Well I guess you can do them forever. I suppose that's how anyone gets famous nowadays – you do one thing till you get noticed for it, and you don't stop even when it's boring you to death – you have to go on and on with the same thing until finally you're *a household name* . . . which, now that excellence has lost its meaning, is all we've got left to aspire to.

Beat.

Thanks for coming over here. Your place is great but . . . you know.

Jean   It's not clean.

Andy   Well, I don't wanna seem crazy or anything but I think hygiene is important.

Jean   I can see that, yeah.

Andy   So who wants to start?

Silence. They look at the blank canvas.

Jean   Weren't you going to –?

Andy   Well, it was just a suggestion.

Jean   No, it's what you do. It's your thing, you know. So I think we should start with that.

Andy   Okay. I need *some*thing to work off.

Jean   Cool. Let's do that.

Andy   Okay.

Jean   So what do you –?

Andy   I have my thing here. My little *machine*. My little tracing machine.

Andy *begins to set up the tracing projection machine, (downstage centre) points it out into the auditorium, then finds the right slide.*

What he has here is a device that can project images onto the blank canvas so the artist can trace the outline.

Andy   I just got a new one. It's so great. You just choose your image and hey presto.

Jean (*firmly*)   And then you're going to paint by hand?

Pause. **Andy** *stares at* **Jean**.

Andy   Well I . . . I dunno . . . I guess. I mean I *could*. But I haven't painted by hand in twenty-five years.

Jean   I, I, I just think, you know, it would help make your style and mine, you know . . . fit together more.

Andy   Right.

Jean   Because we –

Andy   We're very different. (*Pause.*) I know. I was worried about that too. You're all spontaneous and wild . . . and so deep and mystical and I'm . . . while I'm still a commercial illustrator really, a photographer, obsessed with the surface of things. And –

Jean   Don't you need a new challenge? And you can't just screen print your life away, you know.

Andy   Can't I? I was planning to. But maybe you're right.

Jean   You need to start painting again. You know? How can you call yourself a painter if you, you know, never paint?

Andy   I don't call myself a painter.

Jean   Well, how can you call yourself the greatest artist in the world?

Andy   Never said that either. Maybe *the most famous*, but . . . Okay, I'll try. See, I had an idea of how this might work, how me might, you know, collaborate together. So I have a slide here . . . of the logo of . . . let's see if it works . . . I thought it was just great . . . if I can get it to work . . .

He turns on the machine, and the projector beams light into the auditorium. Both men step downstage and stare out into space, as if at the image.

Jean *is unimpressed.*

Jean   General Electric?

Andy   I love it. Don't you?

Jean *just stares at it.*

Jean   A logo? Of General Electric?

Andy   What do you think? I mean, it has to work for both of us. Jean? What do you think? Be honest. We need to be honest with each other if this is going to be interesting.

Jean *looks at it a while, then –*

Andy   You hate it.

Silence.

You don't say much, do you? You hate it.

Jean   No.

Andy   Then what do you think?

Jean   Nothing. I don't think anything.

Andy   Well that's just *great*, right?

Pause.

Jean   Sure, look, whatever. Let's do it. We have to start somewhere.

Andy   Is it that bad?

Jean   You start, get the corporation logo down – sketch the outline – maybe I can help you fill it in, we can both, you know . . . fill it in together –

Andy   Sure, like a colouring book! This might be fun! You know those were the first things I ever did when I was sick as a child, with my mother.

Jean   Let's do that then, you know. And then maybe I'll paint some things in the spaces, around it, or on top of it.

Andy   On top of it? You're going to overpaint me?

Jean   Let's see. I'm relaxed, you know. Whatever comes up. I don't think we should think too much about it. Just see what comes up *naturally*. Let inspiration happen, you know.

Andy   Naturally? Okay, if you're sure. Alright, well . . .

As **Jean** *takes out a packet of jelly snakes and starts to eat one,* **Andy** *goes to the canvas and takes a pencil and is about to draw his first line, but then stops –*

Andy   Gee, I'm nervous. How great is that? My hand is shaking. It's been so long, you know, since I've drawn anything coz I usually get my assistant to do this part. Oh, Jean, maybe you should do this bit? And I'll do some, I dunno some stretches to get warmed up. I'm so stiff. Like a corpse.

Jean   Maybe you should smoke a joint.

Andy   No, but thank you, no. It's so strange.

Beat.

Maybe we should take a break, you know. For coffee or something. You wanna coffee? Or maybe we've even done enough for today. What do you think?

Jean   Andy, you've just turned on the projector.

Andy *is genuinely nervous about this.*

Andy   I don't know what's wrong with me. Okay then. I guess. Well, here goes. What's the worst that can happen?

Andy, *facing upstage, away from the audience now, traces, onto a large white frames canvas (centre-stage) the projected image of the*

GE logo. The audience is thus able to watch the creation of an art work in real time.

Andy   Talk to me, while I work. Distract me.

Jean   Distract you from what?

Andy   Tell me, something. Anything.

Pause

Jean   Why General Electric?

Andy   It's a . . . it's a huge company.

Jean   A huge *boring* company. I mean, what's with all the, all the corporations? Campbell's Soup can't get by without you? The dollar bill need you? Coke? Don't they, you know, have enough money, power?

Andy   That's the point. Soon they'll have *all* the power. The time's coming, Jean, when the Campbell's Soup Company will own *everything*. There'll just be, like, three or four huge companies, like Campbell's or Coke, and we'll all be serving them.

Jean   Sounds like a good reason *not* to paint their logos. Unless we're gonna pull them down, you know. Bring 'em down in some way. Criticise them, you know? They're the enemy, man. Don't you have to make some, you know, *comment*?

Andy   But I *am* commenting. *In a neutral way.* No one ever gets this but I'm . . . it's hard to understand . . . well I'm trying to make art that . . . that forces you to ignore it . . . the same way we're ignoring life . . . I think that's honest, you know. More and more we're ignoring everything, so why not 'ignorable art'? Why not the 'ignorable artist'? That's why I use techniques like screen-printing that don't even need an artist. Some shitty critic recently called me 'Nothingness Himself' – like it was a bad thing!

Beat.

You know, Jean, by making me do this by hand, you're really jeopardising my entire manifesto. I'm gonna have my grubby little prints all over this thing.

Jean That's one weird theory of art, man.

Andy Do you think so?

Jean It can't be about *nothing*, man. And I don't mean art has to be about *something*, but it has to have some kind of function, a *purpose*.

Andy Gee. You see, I disagree with that. Why can't it just be about nothing . . . (*Looks at* **Jean**.) for nobodies?

Jean *laughs, enjoying this sparring match.*

Jean You're succeeding. It's working!

Andy (*sensing a slight*) Wow.

Jean And as for us becoming servants of corporations. Maybe. Sure. But I think art, you know, should stand up against all that. Fuck that, you know. All these, you know, brand names. They're like the devil. World's like one huge brand now . . .

Andy One of the things I hope history will remember me for, if there's any justice, is that I've broken down the walls between business and art. Business *is* art, it's the best art. And art has *always* been business. It's all commerce now. And I did that . . . shoot me. I really need to stop saying that. It's like I'm asking for it. Anyway, we're not painters anymore, Jean. We're *brands*. Well, you're *almost* a giant brand, and after this exhibition with me you will be too. Then just watch the language change, Jean. People will have to '*have you*' suddenly . . . And not you. Not you. Your *paintings*. 'Have a Basquiat . . . I have to *have* him. I need him.' So when they '*want you*', when strangers say they '*want you*', Jean, '*desire you*', Jean, '*love you*', all they'll mean is they want a silly painting of yours . . . You'll be invisible, a brand. You'll finally, triumphantly, cease to exist. As we appropriate, we are appropriated. Voila: *Nothingness Himself*.

Jean   So, everything means nothing, and so art should mean nothing?

Andy   Everything's just surfaces now. Right? Nobody means anything they say anymore. Right? Everything's turning into a lie.

Beat.

Let's lighten the mood. Tell me what you did last night? What did you do last night, Jean? Anything interesting?

Jean   I found a dead body on my front step.

Andy   Of course you did.

Jean   Dead guy.

Andy   God, you need to get out of the East Village, Jean. It's a jungle down there. What did you do with the body? Did you bury it?

Jean   I called the cops. A wino had, you know, a heart attack.

Andy   Heart attacks are terrible. There's no warning at all. Apparently you're great, then – (*Slaps his chest hard.*) – oblivion.

Jean (*sarcastic*)   Just some tramp.

Andy   Did you film it? The dead body? You should have filmed it. That would have been *great*.

Beat.

God I hope this logo looks good. I don't want it to look *messy*.

Jean   Messy is good. Messy is real. Life is messy.

Andy   That's exactly what I'm worried about.

Jean *sits on the couch and rolls a joint . . .*

Jean   So . . . what did *you* do last night?

Andy Me?

Jean Yeah. What did you do last night?

Andy Me? Oh. God. Well I . . . I went out early. Took all my old bread to the park . . . to feed the pigeons . . . but they didn't come around and I just hated them for that.

Jean (*laughs*) That was it? That was all Andy Warhol did?

Andy *is provoked to be more generous now.*

Andy Ah. Yeah. Well no . . . actually it turned into a kinda interesting night. After the park I uh . . . I paid a quick visit to my church because I missed Mass the day before . . . then walking home I bumped into Mapplethorpe. He's either lost his looks, or he's sick, then I . . . then I got dressed and took a cab, five dollars, and went to an early party at Yoko's for little Sean's birthday . . . and the funniest thing happened . . . I went into Sean's bedroom and he was with this kid who was connecting up one of these new home computer things, an Apple, the Mcintosh model, and I told them that, oh, a man had once called me *a lot,* wanting to give me one, but that I never called him back or something, and this kid, this friend of Sean's looked up at me and said, 'Yeah, that was me, I'm Steve Jobs.' And he looked so young! Like a college guy. And he gave me a lesson on drawing on it, but it's only black and white at this point but who knows in the future. So from there I got a limo, fifteen dollars, to Mick and Jerry's for dinner on West 81st Street. There were three butch bodyguards outside, who travel everywhere with Mick and who I guess have no lives of their own. Jack Nicholson was there. He's fat now which is a shame. Jerry's pregnant and if it's a boy I'm sure Mick will marry her at last. Oh, and Salvador was there, *Dali,* eccentric as ever, pretending he doesn't speak English when everyone knows perfectly well he can. And from there, umm, oh yeah, I walked over to have late cocktails with Princess Gloria von Thurn und Taxis and her husband Johannes I think his name is, who told me this amazing story that when he was young he went to

Hollywood and met, get this, he met Marilyn Monroe and that she came on to him and invited him for dinner but he said he wasn't into women then – and he said this *out loud* – they talk like that – his wife talking about *boys* and he talking about *boys with big cocks*. I guess that passes for European sophistication now. So anyway, he said that he'd asked Marilyn who else was going to be at dinner and she said a bunch of names and when he arrives Marilyn comes out in a *décolleté negligee* and he said 'where are the other people?' and she said 'they all cancelled' and so they had pink champagne and dinner and then she pulled a little string and she was standing there stark naked and he just *couldn't* . . . so he said he just banged one out on her knockers then said 'see ya later toots.' She must've known how rich he was, it's the only explanation. Anyway, I bid them goodbye and Gloria wanted a cock drawn on her copy of *Interview* magazine, of course with my signature because everyone's wised up now, and . . . and by this time the pain in my side was killing me, I've had this, this pain in my side, so I cabbed it, six, seven dollars, to an all-night drug store and got some Valium and aspirin coz I was out. Valium's my new thing now. And I went home and no one had fed the dogs. I slept like a baby. And that was it. You?

Beat.

And you, Jean? (*Beat.*) After you got rid of the corpse? They tell me you have a lot of girlfriends now. A ladies man. How many? Two, three, four? Do they have names?

Silence.

Andy   Now look, you can't just let me do all the talking. Okay?

Beat.

It's not fair. *I* usually play the silent enigmatic one.

Jean   You should see a doctor. About that pain, you know. Either the pancreas or the gall bladder.

Andy   Oh I'm seeing Dr Li, with her Chinese cures, and I'm doing shiatsu. Hopefully just a muscle spasm, but if it's not I'm a goner.

Jean   See a regular doctor.

Andy   Over my dead body. Now talk. Tell me about your girlfriends?

Jean   Why are you so silent in interviews? One word answers and stuff.

Andy   Oh, well I don't want *everyone* to think I'm a homo. When I open my mouth I give the game away. I can't afford that. Now come on.

Jean *smiles, then finally –*

Jean   Maya. Her name's Maya. Okay? Who I'm seeing right now.

Andy   Maya. Sounds like trouble.

Jean   She's wonderful. Beautiful person. Has a soul. Ancient soul.

Andy *plunges his now blunt pencil into an automatic pencil sharpener . . . grrrrrrrr . . .*

Jean   Who are *you* seeing? Tell me about your boyfriends.

Andy   I bet they're all in love with you.

Jean   They maybe think they are. But it's mainly just an image of me they have. There's something about me, I dunno, that makes people feel protective of me in some way, you know?

Andy, *lonely, reflects on this.*

Andy   And who else?

Jean *smokes the joint.*

Jean   Others. A few others.

Andy   Bruno says you're fucking Madonna.

Jean *coolly smokes and doesn't like to confirm this –*

Jean   You want some? (*Joint.*)

Andy   No. And if you don't mind, I don't like to see drugs in my studio and I like even less to smell them. Now you have to bring her down here. I'd like to film her. Tape her.

Jean   Why do you like to record everyone?

Andy   I prefer everything to be a movie.

Jean   Can I ask you something? Why are you so white?

Andy (*shocked*)   Oh.

Jean   You're so white. Man. I can't believe I'm hanging around with someone so white. How did you get so white?

Andy   I'm white because I was a hypersensitive child and I lost my pigment at eight. I was henceforward known by the other kids as Spot. Gosh, I wish people wouldn't go on about my looks. I wish more people were blind.

Andy *works, slow to respond.* **Jean** *walks away, losing interest in the answer, going to get something to eat.*

Andy *finishes the pencilling, and steps back to look at the projected image with his pencil outlines.*

Andy   There. That should give me the idea anyway. What do you think? Jean? Come and look. What do you think?

Jean *is looking at a Campbell's soup can picture in a large art book.*

Jean   Repetition.

Andy   Mmm?

Jean   You like repetition.

Andy   Two Liza Minnellis, ten Elizabeth Taylors, thirty-six Elvises, 102 Troy Donahues.

Jean   By repeating things, maybe, you're trying to kill them, make them lose their power.

Andy   That's interesting. Do you think so? Well, when you see anything over and over I guess it loses its power. Like auto accidents. And husbands.

Jean   You want to kill soup. You're trying to kill soup.

Andy   Come and look at this. I guess you should fill this in now.

Jean   How did you come up with this? The soup cans? How did you come up with this Campbell's soup idea? Were you stoned? Were you high?

Andy   Oh that was my mother. That was my mother's idea.

Jean   It was? Ha! Ha! Ha! Really? Ha! Ha! Ha!

Andy   The whole soup cans thing.

Jean   Really? Your mother? How, how, so how did that, y'know – how did that –?

Andy   Happen?

Jean   Yeah how did *that* happen. Ha! Ha! Ha!

Andy   She was . . . well I was . . . I was doing all these different things, cartoon paintings of Nancy and Dick Tracy with speech bubbles but Lichtenstein stole this whole cartoon idea from me, so I was too late to that party, and I was just very depressed and mother was living with me by then and we were in my kitchen and I told her I've got to do something that really will have a lot of impact but will be different enough from Lichtenstein and Rosenquist, and she said, 'Andy, you should do pictures of things that are recognisable to everyone.' And I said what and she said, 'Yes, like this . . . like this soup can here for example.' So I looked at the soup can, I had soup every day for lunch, but I kept looking at it, deeper and deeper and then I *saw* it . . . I saw it for the first time. I saw its *essence*. It was still just a soup can but it was also now America. *My* America, my *mother's* America, the one she'd come from Czechoslovakia to discover. The history of this country, in a soup can. See, I tried to let the things that would ordinarily bore me, thrill me, and when I did good things happened. I *also* learned that genius entails luck: right place, right time, right people, right lunch.

Andy *is done. He looks at the sketch.*

Andy   Now that's about as good as I do. What shall we do for paint? Are we gonna do things like *mix colours*? I hope not. You'll have to do that, Jean. There's only so much you can ask of me.

Jean   Why don't we just use the colours we have and just see what happens. That's what I do. Straight out of the tin, guerrilla style. On the street there's never any time to mix anything because the cops might show up at any second.

Andy   Ah ha!

Jean *goes to the tins of paints.*

Jean   Here's some stuff I was using yesterday, let's just go with that. What colour you wanna start with?

Andy   Well, the GE logo is blue, I'm pretty sure. Wait, you were painting *yesterday*?

Jean   Uh huh.

Andy   And how about the day before that?

Jean   Sure.

Andy   Oh that's terrific. You're really on fire, Jean. I'm so jealous. I used to be like that.

Jean *hands* **Andy** *the small paint tin.*

Jean   So. Here. Try this. Doesn't matter if it's the wrong shade.

Andy   Me?

Jean   Yeah, the logo is your thing.

Andy   Well, what do I put it on with?

Jean   Here . . .

Jean *gets him a paint brush, and puts it in his other hand.*

Jean   It's called a brush.

Andy *looks at the paintbrush as if it's an alien object.*

Andy   One of *these*. Achh, I remember these.

Jean (*trying to understand the reluctance*)   What?

Andy *reluctantly picks up the paint now and then pauses before dipping the brush in the paint. Finally does so. But then pauses again, reluctant to set brush to canvas . . .*

Jean   Do it. Andy! What's wrong? DO IT!

Andy   Ugh.

Andy *begins to colour in the GE logo . . .*

Jean *turns on a tape of Miles Davis . . . Miles' 'Flamenco Sketches' for a few bars, before he changes it to the frenetic 'Turnaroundphrase – Live at the Newport Jazz Festival, Berlin'.*

Andy   The end of twenty-five years of celibacy.

Andy *struggles to concentrate . . . as* **Jean** *dances and grooves to the music.*

Jean   Why'd you stop believing in painting?

Beat.

How come?

Andy *paints . . . won't answer this question.*

Andy   Bruno says . . . You know . . . Bruno says my problem . . .

Andy *stops painting.*

Andy   . . . is that I can't return love. What do you think? Is he right?

Jean   I don't know you, Andy. Keep colouring.

Andy *tries to paint while talking* . . .

Andy   I remember when Valerie shot me . . . she told someone she did it 'out of love'. She loved me, and so when I didn't love her back, *bang bang bang*. Lou Reed said I deserve all I get, including being shot. I'm starting to really hate Lou now. Everybody seems to want things from me I never promised to give them.

Jean   Do you think you're cold?

Andy   Do I? Oh, gee, I don't know. Getting shot by a friend doesn't exactly make you wanna run around shouting the L-word from the rooftops.

Jean   So you connect the L-word . . . love, with death?

Andy   Jesus didn't die on the cross because he couldn't pay the rent. Would you mind if we switched to classical music? Anything?

Jean   How come?

Andy   Jean, please. I can't work like this.

Jean *shrugs, can't see what the big issue is, but goes to change the tape. The classical music starts (Ravel's 'Boléro', a* **Jean** *favourite) then* **Jean** *comes back to see how* **Andy**'s *painting is going* . . .

Jean   See? I told you. You still got it. You could even become a great graffiti artist. It's not too late, you know.

Andy   I don't know how you do it. How do you deal with all the emotions that come up when you paint?

Jean   Andy, you're colouring in the General Electric logo.

Andy   Easy for you to say.

Jean   You didn't answer my question by the way. Bruno said you don't believe in painting anymore.

Andy (*shrugs*)   I do art. And I do art because I'm ugly and there's nothing else for me to do.

Jean   And what would you do if you were better looking?

Andy   Oh God, *anything*!

Jean   I don't think you're bad looking.

Andy *stares at* **Jean**, *moved by this.*

Andy   You don't?

Jean   You look fine. No one is ugly anyway. Only what some people *do* is ugly. Or what they think.

Andy   Here – you come and do some now. This is too much.

Jean *picks up the paintbrush and begins to effortlessly colour in the 'General Electric' logo.*

Andy *turns off the classical music.*

Andy   You're so much better. I want to film you . . .

Jean   No. Andy. No. I don't want that.

Andy *picks up his film camera and starts to film* **Jean** . . .

Andy   I want to make a film of our collaboration. You have to let me. (*Narrating.*) 'So, here we find Jean-Michel Basquiat, the hottest new artist in New York and possibly the world, at work. Say hello, Jean. Say hello.'

Jean   Come on, Andy.

Andy   Now Jean, can you tell us, tell posterity, why do *you* do art? Jean? Why do you do art? Jean, come on . . .

Jean   To eat. I dunno. It's . . . I guess . . . it's the one thing they let me get away with. They don't let someone like me get away with very much, you know.

Andy   So . . . art now is simply what you get away with? That's great.

Jean   There's no rules, right? In the . . . in the old days, of Rembrandt, you know, and, and, and Da Vinci, you know, who I think is probably my favourite painter, art was . . . well it was something everyone looked at, you know, and said 'well *I* couldn't do that'. It automatically got respect for that reason, you know. But *contemporary* art, you look at it and everyone just says, 'I could do that. I *didn't*, but I *could*.' And they're right. So the value now has to come from, you know, the market . . . the market, you know, telling people what's good, what's *valuable*, what's investable. So we got Michael, my friend Michael Stewart, who is just as good as I am, out there on the streets right now, probably getting hassled by the cops for like the thousandth time for spraying stuff on a wall, but otherwise *invisible*, you know, invisible forever . . . while we, you and me, are in here killing soup . . . just so we can sell dead soup to the CEO of General Electric who will love that we put his logo in one our famous valuable paintings. And *that* . . . that's the art market!

Andy   That's so terrific.

Jean   And that's why I hate it. And why I need it. And why I hate it. And why I need it. And why I hate it. And why I need it, can you turn the camera off now? It's creeping me out.

Andy   Sure. (*Keeps filming, but filming the art now.*) Okay.

Jean *paints*.

Jean   Do you think I'm a better painter than Julian?

Andy   Schnabel?

Jean   I think I'm better than everybody, including you.

Andy   That's so macho. You should watch it.

Jean   I've challenged Julian to a boxing match. I want to knock him out.

Andy Careful. He's bigger than you and he doesn't smoke dope.

Jean I'll go into training. Like Sugar Ray . . .

He starts to float, and spar in the air like a boxer to the classical music . . .

Jean . . . like Ali, man . . . watch out . . . like Joe Louis . . . and the earth was formless and void and darkness was on the face of the deep . . . boom! . . . and then there was light and God looked at the light and said that it was good . . . boom! . . . and the spirit moved across the water . . . boom! . . . and nicotine walks on eggshells medicated . . . copywright J.M. Basquiat . . . *boom* . . . breathing in his lungs 2000 years of asbestos . . . boom! boom! . . .

Jean *comes intimately close to* **Andy**.

Jean . . . Boom for real.

Andy, *moved by this intimacy, also cannot cope with it. Continues filming.*

Andy Tell me about Madonna. Are you fucking her?

Jean Andy. Come on.

Andy I'm amazed you don't have children littered all across New York.

Jean I have one, in New Orleans. I look after him and his mother.

Andy This is important. Tell me who you most admire – living painters you admire?

Jean Turn it off. Or I'm going.

Andy Don't be so selfish, Jean. This is an important historical record. So what living painters do you most admire? Come on.

The doorbell buzzes: brrrrrr . . . brrrrrrrr . . .

Jean Julian. It's bad luck to film.

Andy You're so superstitious.

Jean You go to church. Why go to church? That's superstitious.

Andy To pray.

Jean Does it work, when you pray?

Andy I don't know if it works, but it doesn't *not* work.

Beat.

I'm fundamentally a disbeliever whose disbelief regularly fails. Is there a God? Well, it's good insurance to act as if there is.

Beat.

And who else? Painters you love?

Jean Julian. Francesco Clemente . . . Sandro Chia . . . Twombly most of all.

Andy And whose art do you *hate* the most?

Jean Julian. Francesco Clemente, Sandro Chia, Twombly most of all.

Enter **Bruno** *with a bag of doughnuts.*

Bruno Doughnuts!

Andy *is annoyed.*

Andy Bruno!

Bruno What?

Andy You can't be here when we work!

Jean (*relaxed*) Hey, Bruno.

Bruno Not staying. Not staying. Just dropping off food.

Jean *grabs the bag of doughnuts and exits the room.* **Andy** *turns off his camera, frustrated.*

Bruno   So. How's it going?

Andy   Oh it's going great and yeah, it was kinda hard to get him talking at first but I finally did it, I finally got him to open up, then you will never guess what happened?

Bruno (*excited*)   Oh God, what?

Andy   Then you walked in the room and fucked everything up!

Bruno   I just brought doughnuts.

Andy   Do I look like I eat doughnuts? Get out!

Bruno   But really, how's it going? You and Jean? It's working out, yes?

Andy   Well, I don't understand him. How he works, what his process is, what his art is trying to do or say, and when I ask him about it he won't talk. Other than that, *great*.

As **Andy** *reloads the camera.*

Bruno   Okay Andy, let me talk to him –

Jean *enters, eating a doughnut.*

Bruno   This is so exciting! (*Going to* **Jean**.) Incredible already. (*Aside, to* **Jean**.) So?

Jean   What?

Bruno   So?

Jean   He just wants to film me all the time.

Bruno   When he's excited, he films. He'll calm down.

Jean   And he won't paint anything. You wanted a boxing match, can't even get him in the ring! What happened to him? Why is he so weird about painting?

Bruno   Just play along. Give him something, he'll give back. You've *got* this. He's there for the taking!

Andy   Oh Bruno, *you're* still here!

Bruno   Gone. Gone. (*To* **Andy**.) Have a doughnut, they're delicious.

Exit **Bruno**. **Andy** *starts to film* **Jean** *again*.

Andy   So. Jean . . . so Jean, you were like this hot street artist. Why did you stop doing works in the street? Doing graffiti, and those great little cards.

Jean   Hunger.

Andy   Oh, hunger.

Jean   And that was a long time ago, you know. I'm not that person anymore, you know. Why did you stop doing illustrations of women's shoes?

Andy   How did you get into doing street art?

Jean *goes and picks up the joint he put out and re-lights it and takes some more puffs . . .*

Jean   I got a Fulbright . . . to deface New York. No. Some friends from high school and some other kids . . . we just used to drift downtown all the time and write stuff on the walls you know and throw bottles. Just teenage, teenage stuff.

Andy   And you were working under the name Samo. (*Sam-O.*)

Jean (*correcting pronunciation*)   Samo. (*Same-Oh.*)

Andy   Same-Oh?

Jean   It's short for Same-Old-Shit.

Andy   And what made you wanna be a painter in the first place?

Jean   I dunno . . . Getting run over by a car.

Andy   Getting run over by a car? That's so grrreat.

Jean   Yeah.

Andy   Oh, I hope it was a Ford.

Jean   When I was seven years old. Boom. For real. Smashed me up. In hospital my mother brought me a copy of Gray's Anatomy, you know, so I could, like, see what was broken, visualise the bones and the organs and stuff, and voodoo my way with magic back to health.

Andy   Did it work?

Jean   I'm here.

Andy   You really *are* superstitious.

Jean   Isn't everyone?

Andy   No.

Jean   So . . . I had all these injuries from being run over, you know. And I started drawing internal organs and skeletons of the body and . . . and the doctors couldn't believe how fast I recovered.

Andy   And how do you explain that?

Jean   You can't. Shouldn't try. It's a mystery and you need to respect it and leave it alone.

Beat.

Are you going to finish the colouring?

Andy   You're so much better at it. Keep going.

Jean *returns to finishing the colouring in.*

Andy   So that's where all that comes from – the skulls and skeletons and death. Do you think the best art comes out of suffering?

Jean   I . . . I dunno, you know. Who knows where it comes out of.

Andy   Because I reject this idea that who suffers most is the best. What makes you great is your gift. Still, you got really lucky by being hit by that car . . . and, even better, you were black, and on top of that . . . from Haiti, an immigrant treated like shit.

Jean   No man, I was born here. I was born here. Don't say that. I'm *American*.

Andy   So am I, but I'm also a Czech, in my blood.

Jean   No man, you can't say that. I'm a New Yorker. Brooklyn, that's it. The Republic of Brooklyn. My parents just happened to be from Puerto Rico and Haiti.

Andy   And yet here you are, from such humble beginnings – well your dad was an accountant, you lived in a brownstone and you went to a private school but I *love* the whole 'humble' thing – and now you're on the verge of becoming the first really great black painter America has ever seen.

Jean   Fuck that, man. I'm the first really great painter *America* has ever seen.

Andy   That's wonderful. Say it again. Say it again, Jean. Straight into the camera. Straight into the camera. Right into the lens . . .

Jean *walks up to the camera and looks right into the barrel –*

Jean   *I'm the first really great painter America has ever seen. Boom for real.*

Andy   Oh, that was sooo . . . (*Checking camera.*) . . . oh no! I just ran out of film! I don't think I got that last bit. That was the best part.

But **Jean** *grabs the camera. They both have hold of it . . .*

Jean   No. No more filming.

Andy   Jean, let go.

Jean   We're supposed to be painting together. And this is your part of the painting.

Andy   Let go of the camera.

Jean   Not until you help me finish your part. I'll help you.

Andy   That's priceless! But okay.

Andy *lets go of the camera and* **Jean** *puts it away.*

Andy   But then you have to let me film you saying that last part, about you being the greatest. That was *terrific.*

Jean *hands* **Andy** *a brush.*

Jean   Maybe.

Andy   Oh God. Here we go again.

Andy *goes back to look at the unfinished painting.*

Andy   It's really got something.

Jean   For a boring logo.

Andy   But I'm really liking that it's hand painted, even though it goes against everything I stand for. Maybe you're teaching me something new.

Jean   Who knows, you know. (*Annoyed.*) So, Andy –

Andy   Uh huh? What?

Jean *subtly begins to bait* **Andy***, setting a trap . . .*

Jean   If the artist is soon going to, you know, be nothing but a brand . . .

Andy   – a commodity – I pioneered that.

Andy *begins to think he's won* **Jean** *over and has turned* **Jean** *into an acolyte.*

Jean   – and paintings are going to be about nothing more than, you know, money . . . and the best things to paint are boring things like logos and labels . . .

Andy   – that can be mass-produced, preferably by assistants –

Jean   – and all that a painting is meant to do now is . . . what? What's a painting meant to do now?

Andy   Give you a nice little hit, like when you pass a celebrity in the street.

Jean   Okay, and there's nothing, you know, *spiritual* in it, right? . . .

Andy   No, no – God no – it's about *surfaces* now, nothing behind it. Because then we're facing the facts of existence these days. More and more it's just surface existence, with nothing behind it.

Jean   – and soon three giant corporations will run everything –

Andy   – a giant apparatus –

Jean   – where all human activity, no matter how, you know, *sacred*, is –

Andy   – is turned over to the marketplace, that's right –

Jean   – and this apparatus will rule our lives and, you know, hypnotise us into a state of, like, what? Complete permanent televised stupidity –

Andy   I'm just the messenger. Shoot me –

Jean   – then what's left? If all *that* is coming, what's left, man? Andy? You know? What's *left*?

Andy *finally realises he is being baited.*

Jean   You're the prophet. What's left?

Silence, then –

Andy (*pointedly*)   Trash.

Beat.

Trash. But we have to celebrate *something*.

Andy *gestures at* **Jean** . . . *then resumes painting, with a feint, victorious smile on his lips.*

Lights dim.

Act Two

Scene One

Basquiat's Loft Apartment/Studio, Great Jones St, East Village, NY

Bruno *talks on a phone with a very long stretchy-cord. Under his arm, a rolled poster.*

We are in **Jean**'s *studio now. In contrast to* **Andy**'s *it is a pigsty, a mess – an old couch, a coffee table, a TV, a fridge covered in* **Jean**'s *doodles, are variously arranged, paint spattered everywhere, art work on the floor.*

Seven large canvases are covered with sheets. As **Bruno** *speaks on the phone he walks around and pulls the sheets off the seven collaboration canvases.*

Bruno . . . Mary, no, listen, Mary, okay? I'm sending over a draft copy of the poster because . . . the greatest news . . . Tony, *Tony Shafrazi will do the show* . . . Ja, he's agreed . . . Ja ja, he's hyper-ventilating, he'll show everything, all fifteen, fifteen major pieces from these last three years, and today I hope they finish the last one. Shafrazi's is so perfect. Ja ja, no, on West 26th. (*Beat.*) Look, I know you still think I'm making a terrible mistake with their careers, ja ja, but Tony's no fool. I told you, what I have these guys doing, never been done before! I'm telling you Mary, in my chest? I know it, *I am right, I am right, I am right!* This show, the most exciting show in the history of contemporary art for sure.

Bruno *picks up a woman's high-heel shoe off the floor. It looks like a scene of passion has been interrupted here. He sets the shoe on the coffee table.*

No, no. Don't worry, trust me.

Bruno *sits on the couch, and finds a syringe.*

Listen to me. Listen. To. Me. One second. One second.

He thinks about what he should do with the syringe, and puts it on the coffee table.

Enter **Andy**, *through the front door. He's wearing a different wig, even more zany.*

Bruno   I have to go. (*To* **Andy**.) Mary says Hi. (*To* **Mary**.) Okay. Bye.

Andy   Hi and bye, Bruno.

Bruno   It won't take a second.

Andy   You know the rules.

Bruno   One second. The poster. For the show. I need your sign-off, Andy. If you will just approve it.

Andy   What can I smell? I really don't think I can work here one day longer.

Bruno   Andy, the poster – what do you think of it? I think it's so amusing. So witty and charming. Really. Really great.

Andy   What can I smell? It's not dope, is it?

Bruno   Don't you think it's charming? Two boxers? Pugilists in art?

Andy   You can't be here when we work, Bruno. When Jean and I are working you can't be here. (*Looking around.*) How can Jean *live* like this? Let alone work?

Bruno   But I need your approval on the poster. Can we go with it? Send it out, I mean? I love it so much.

Bruno *holds out the poster and* **Andy** *finally takes it.*

Andy   Oh you love everything, Bruno. It's your Swiss desire to be liked. Which is all connected, you know, with your guilt about staying out of the war and getting fat with everybody else's money. You have to admit it, Bruno.

Bruno   Don't be so bitchy, Andy, you fucking asshole. The poster. We need to start getting it out. Build the excitement. In three weeks we open. Please.

Andy   I. Don't. Care. What is on the poster.

Bruno   You don't? Okay, Fine. Then great.

Bruno *holds out his hand to take the poster but* **Andy** *now looks at the poster closely for the first time . . .*

Bruno   Andy?

Andy (*starting to care*)   Why is . . . why is Jean half-naked and I'm wearing a T-shirt? And my skin is so white. It's not that white, is it? I need to buy a sunlamp. Oh that's right, I didn't want to take my T-shirt off. But I look so anaemic, compared to Jean. God. Look how beautiful he looks compared to me in my fright wig! Bruno, I've lost already. If it's a fight I've lost in the final round.

Bruno   I need an answer, Andy.

Andy   You're rushing me. We're still working on the paintings. We're not even done yet. And you need to know Bruno, this whole thing has cost me.

Bruno   Cost you?

Andy   Making me paint again. I'm furious with you. Now get out of here, Bruno.

Bruno   We have fifteen! Fifteen fabulous canvases this one sixteen. Shafrazi's can only hold sixteen paintings of this size. When you finish this one today the collaboration is done. Done.

Andy   I feel old. Do I look old? Where does time go to? And why does it keep going there? It's all this hanging out with young people.

The door phone buzzer sounds.

Andy   It goes all the time. Non-stop. The poster is fine.

Bruno   Wonderful. Wonderful! I will come back later.

Andy   Do you have to? Please don't. We can't be rushed. We're trying to make art, not sandwiches.

Bruno   Oh Andy –

Andy   Out!

Bruno   I found this . . . in the couch.

Shows him the syringe.

Talk to him. Please. He promised me he stopped. You two are so close now, you ask him what the fuck this is.

Andy *points at the door.* **Bruno** *puts the syringe down on the coffee table and exits.*

Andy *is surprised to see a vacuum cleaner. He can tell it has rarely if ever been used.*

Andy *begins to vacuum, and we hear the machine suck up all sorts of small, hard objects . . . clunk, clunk, clunk . . .*

Through the front door, with her own key – enter **Maya**.

Andy *sees* **Maya**.

Andy   Oh!

Andy *turns off the vacuum.*

Andy   Yes?

Maya   Andy? It's me. Maya. We met at Serendipity.

Andy   Oh. Hi. Did Jean give you a key? He's not here right now. We're supposed to be working.

Maya   He's not here?

Andy   You'll have to come back later.

Maya   He needs to give me money.

Andy   Well, that's what they all say.

Maya   Shit!

Andy   What?

Maya   I'm meeting him here so he can give me money.

Andy   Well, he's not here.

Maya   He's promised me money but I need it now, today, right now Andy, otherwise . . . I have to sell my refrigerator to Christie's so I can make rent and have an abortion. It's his.

Andy   Oh my God. (*Long pause.*) Why will you sell your refrigerator to Christie's?

Maya   Because it's covered in Jean's doodles, all over, words and pictures, and I know now what it's worth. Christie's says a lot of money at auction. Listen, I've got a limousine waiting for me down in the street so if you could hurry up. You have to help me Andy. He's got cash stashed all over the place. He doesn't trust banks.

Andy   You hired a limousine, and you can't pay your rent? That is so extravagant.

Maya   I thought he'd be here and he always gives me cash.

Andy   This is *interesting*. So does, does, does your refrigerator look like this one?

Maya   Better. More doodles. He doodled all over it when he *said* he was in love with me. Little pictures, paintings on it.

Andy   Really?

Beat.

All over.

Maya   Yeah. All over. I sent Christie's a photo and they want to come over right now. I got a photo here.

Andy   You got a photo? Really? Show me.

He looks at the photo.

Andy Oh. That's so great. I love it. Ummm. And you want to sell it. Gee. Maya, okay, so listen . . . where do you live now?

Maya Two blocks over on East 4th. Just two blocks over.

Andy What apartment?

Maya Apartment 5, 426 East 4th.

Andy 426 East 4th.

Maya It's a masterpiece. It'll end up at MOMA or The Whitney, I'm telling ya.

Andy Hmm. I'll tell you what I'm going to do. Jean is busy right now. Something terrible has happened to his friend, Michael.

Maya Michael?

Andy Jean's friend.

Maya Michael *Stewart*?

Andy Ah, yeah. So Jean went –

Maya Oh my God. He's one of my best friends! What happened? Is he okay? What happened?

Andy The police beat him up – choked him with a club for spraying some graffiti in the subway –

Maya The fuckers.

Andy Yeah.

Maya The fucking fuck fuckers.

Andy – then smashed his face through the patrol car window. He's in a coma now down at Bellevue. Jean is down there now.

Maya Same old shit. God! I gotta get down there. Ah, this is all so messed up.

Andy   I'll buy it off you. The refrigerator. Then you can do what you want with the money. How much do you want for it?

Maya   Poor Michael. They can't get away with this.

Andy   I know, I know. But wait.

Maya   What?

Andy   I could buy it from you. The refrigerator.

Maya   The refrigerator? Oh. Well, Christie's said I can easily get eight thousand for a good Basquiat fridge.

Andy   Gee. Eight thousand? For an ice-box? I don't know.

Maya   It still works. The light inside.

Andy   I'll give you five. Okay? Five thousand. But I can't give you eight. That's my best offer.

Maya   Five? Okay. But I need it now.

Andy   Gosh, don't tell Jean I bought it.

Maya   Why should I tell him? It's mine.

Andy   But I don't have any cash on me. I never carry it, it's too dangerous. Go to my office on Broadway and they'll write you a cheque.

Maya   I need cash, Andy. It has to be cash. And I need it now. And then I need to go down to the fucken hospital.

Andy   I don't have cash, I told you.

Maya   Then borrow it from Jean. I gotta go.

Andy   He's not here.

Maya   Have you checked the refrigerator?

Andy   Why should I check the refrigerator?

She crosses the room and opens the ice-box. Thousands of dollars of loose bills cascade out of the fridge and form a pile on the floor.

Andy *stares at the pile.*

Andy   You weren't kidding, he really doesn't trust banks.

Maya   I told you.

Andy   But I don't think I should touch his money.

Maya   You're a millionaire, Andy. You can pay him back. Write *him* a cheque. He'll trust you. And this is an emergency.

Andy   Okay. I guess. *Four* thousand dollars –

Maya   Five thousand.

Andy   But you'll have to count it. I'll check it.

She gets on her knees and starts collecting the cash.

Maya   Okay. But this limousine will be killing me. I haven't got time for this shit.

Andy   Well, the limousine was your idea. How you kids live these days. You simply *refuse* to go without. Does Jean know you're pregnant?

Maya   Yeah. But I can't have a baby with him.

Andy   Why not?

Maya   He's a . . . free spirit. And it's all booked and everything.

Andy   Well, it's your body.

Maya   Last time I checked.

Andy   Jean's crazy keeping all this in the fridge.

Maya   Jean is a beautiful beautiful person, but sometimes . . .

Andy   I can't imagine what it's like to have a relationship with him.

Maya   Have you fucked him yet?

Andy *stares at her, shocked.*

Maya   You guys have been hanging out nearly every night for months, going everywhere together, have you fucked him yet?

Andy   Gosh. You really shouldn't talk like that. It's so trashy.

Maya   He used to be a hustler, when he first came over from Brooklyn, did he tell you?

Andy (*lying*)   Uh huh. Of course he did. But with me he's on his best behaviour.

Maya   Okay. I think I have it. (*The money.*) Do you want to count it?

Andy   I guess I should. Okay.

He takes the cash, and starts to count it.

Maya   Poor Michael. Fuckers.

Andy   Oh my God. I feel like a bank robber! This is so much money. He's really in trouble.

Maya   He sells a painting and they bring him the cash, collectors bring him the cash in, like, these suitcases. It's bad for him, Andy. He's burned out his nose, the inner walls of his nose, with cocaine, and that's why he switched to heroin. Only reason.

Andy   Okay so . . . that's one thousand dollars. So are you . . . are you . . . are you and Jean serious about each other? Are you in love?

Maya   We were, I think . . . I was . . . but Jean . . . he's changed. These last few months . . . something's happening to him. But you should know. *You've* been with him. Look, I got no illusions. He's always seeing lots of women at the same time and he doesn't hide it at least.

Andy   Two thousand.

Maya Some guys, you know, you just have to accept what you're getting into. And if you do, don't complain. He knows he's a fuck up. He doesn't hide it. That's what makes him so loveable. He's so fragile, and vulnerable, and sweet, I just want to run a bath and wash him, scrub him clean, every time I see him. And he loves that . . . being washed . . . especially his hair . . .

Andy Three thousand . . .

She goes to the painting, with the Paramount logo.

Maya And at least he's painting again. He was doing a lot of smack when he was with me. (*Observes.*) And no more skulls. That's a good sign. My fridge is covered in these scary masks. He calls them masks, or helmets or something. He's got a Haitian word for them, gasco, or something. Means helmet.

Andy Four thousand . . . So when can I send someone to come and pick up the refrigerator?

Maya Oh. Anytime. But not today. God, poor Michael. I'm around during the days. I only go out at night. Let me write my phone number down for you. Got a pen?

Andy Somewhere . . . (*Counting cash.*) six, seven, eight . . .

Maya *finds a black pastel marker and then looks for something to write on, settling on the painting.* **Andy** *is too busy counting the cash to notice when* **Maya** *writes her number on the bottom of the painting . . . 2434546.*

Andy . . . ten. God, so much money. Okay. That is –

Andy *sees what she's doing . . .*

Andy What are you doing?! Maya. No! That is sacrilege! You can't *do* that!

Maya It's fine. Jean puts numbers on all his paintings for no apparent reason.

Andy Still!

Maya   He'll paint over it, later, if he doesn't like it. Tell Jean, if I miss him, I've gone down to the hospital to see Michael.

Andy   Your money, here, five thousand. I don't know what I'm gonna tell Jean. If you see him at the hospital tell him I'm here, waiting for him.

Maya   Thanks for the cash. You know Andy, you're okay.

Maya *runs out.* **Andy** *goes to the window, looks out and then returns to the fridge and puts away the cash.*

When **Andy** *is done he begins to explore the apartment. Everything he touches is dirty. He takes out a handkerchief and cleans his hands. He finds a pair of boxing gloves and pulls these on and then goes to look at himself in a mirror, posing . . .*

At this point, we hear the rising noises of an angry argument erupting outside the door – the voices those of **Two Strangers**.

Stranger One (*off*)   Say that again and I'll kill ya!

Stranger Two (*off*)   You piece of shit, I hate you!

Stranger One (*off*)   Say it again! Say it one more time and I swear to God –

Stranger Two (*off*)   You fat pig! Fat Pig! Fat Pig Fat Pig Fat Pig Fat Pig! I hate you! There! What you gonna do now, huh?

A body falls against **Jean**'s *door, rattling it. They are just on the other side of the door.*

Andy, *still wearing the boxing gloves, backs a safe distance away.*

Andy   Hail, Mary, full of grace, the Lord is with thee and blessed art thou among women.

Stranger One (*off*)   What about *this?* Huh?

Stranger Two (*off*)   You're not man enough to use it. G'head. Do it.

Stranger One (*off*)   One more word, see what happens!

Stranger Two (*off*)   You'll never do it! G'head! I dare ya!

BANG! A gun-shot (Off.) And then silence. And then . . .

Andy   My God.

Stranger Two (*off*)   Ha! Ha! Ha! Ha! Shit! You did it!

Stranger One (*off*)   What about that? Huh?

Stranger Two (*off*)   Ha! Ha! Ha! Ha! You did it!

Stranger One (*off*)   Ha! Ha! Ha!

The **Stranger**'s *laughter then trails away as they go up to their own apartment . . .*

When sirens rise **Andy**, *shaken, creeps to the window and looks cautiously down, careful not to show his face.*

Andy   How can anybody work like this? Holy Mary Mother of . . .

Just then . . . the door opens and **Jean** *enters.* **Jean** *is in an agitated state.*

Andy   Jean, get in here! Lock the door. You won't believe what's been going on around here. It's a menagerie!

Beat.

How is he? How's Michael? Jean, is he okay?

Jean   No change.

Jean *goes to* **Andy** *and hugs him. We are now three years into their collaboration and they have grown close.*

Andy   Well, that could be a good thing.

Jean   Still in a coma.

Andy   Look, I think I should go. Today just got way too crazy. But you'll have to walk me out.

Jean   Stay. Andy, please. Stay. His face was all smashed up. All these colours. Not just black and blue. Purples, pinks, greens, red, yellow. Like a mask. Please stay. I don't wanna be alone.

Andy   Well . . . maybe . . . but don't expect me to work.

Jean   You want some champagne?

Andy   What?

Jean   Cristal. I got a few boxes of it somewhere.

Andy   Champagne? Now? God no.

Jean *pulls out a bottle of champagne.*

Andy *takes off the boxing gloves.*

Jean   Here. Come on. Andy? It's supposed to be the best.

Jean *gives* **Andy** *the unopened bottle.*

Andy   Jean, I have a confession to make. I spent five thousand dollars of your money.

Jean   Whatever.

Andy   I'll have someone bring it to you in cash tomorrow.

Jean   I don't care. It's cool, you know.

Andy   My God of course I will. And don't you want to know what I spent it on?

Jean   No.

Andy   Okay.

Jean *goes up to the Paramount picture and writes two words over* **Andy**'s *work . . . Graffiti-like . . . PIR NEMA.*

Andy   You can work with all this stuff going on? What's that? Pir . . .?

Jean   Nema . . .

Andy *takes out his Super 16 film camera and loads it with film.*

Jean   Michael's been going around writing that on walls all around the East Village. It means 'my name'. Then they, you know, they caught him in the subway. They said he was spraying.

Andy *quickly loads the camera, eager to film this . . .*

Andy   And they . . . they . . . they let you . . . in to see him?

Jean   Cops everywhere. The cops are worried about an investigation. They questioned me, all these things, if Michael was violent and stuff.

Andy *raises the camera to begin filming but when* **Jean** *continues speaking . . . he respectfully now lowers it again, despite being sorely tempted . . .*

Jean   I demanded to know what had happened to him, you know, and they said he'd resisted arrest by five officers. Little Michael, resisting five officers. Can you imagine Michael being able to fight off five New York cops? And then the doctor came up and said to Michael's mother, 'There are so many things wrong with your son, Ma'am, we're not sure where to start.' That's what he said.

Jean *looks up, into* **Andy**'s *face.*

Andy   Gee. I'm so sorry to hear that.

Jean   He's had, like, a huge haemorrhage at the base of his brain that the doctor said came from being strangled, you know. The cops strangled him with a billy club. Then broke the back window of the police car with his face. The doctor let me in to see him. Tubes coming out of every part of him, unrecognisable. I took some . . . some Polaroids . . . pulled back the . . . the sheet and took . . . evidence . . .

He takes out three Polaroids from his jacket and hands them to **Andy**.

Jean   It's Michael. But you can't tell. Bruises, cuts all over, lacerations from the handcuffs, same on his . . . on his feet, they shackled him, like a slave. His face and hair still have small pieces of glass stuck in them . . .

Andy, *with his free hand, sneakily reaches for, and raises the camera again, but once more lowers it when* **Jean** *continues.*

Jean   They used his face to smash the window, then choked him damn near to death. For doing some graffiti. Writing some poetry on a subway wall. Always wrote poetry.

Beautiful things. Wanting to be like me, imitating me, hoping one day he'd get famous, like me. Little Jean, they call him.

Andy   Do you think he's gonna make it?

Jean (*convinced*)   Yes.

Beat.

You hungry? Andy? I got . . .

Jean *goes to the fridge. When he opens the door cash spills out again. He ignores the cash, and takes out – caviar.*

I've got caviar if you want it. You want caviar? I just spent three thousand on caviar.

Andy   You can't keep spending money like that. You never know when your fortunes might turn. Honestly.

Jean *turns on jazz, as* **Andy** *watches, then – sets up an easel and energetically places a smaller canvas upon it, then – prepares the tools he'll need and starts a new painting . . .*

Andy *knows enough to say nothing, as he resumes filming this natural talent in full flow . . .*

Jean *works aggressively on this smaller, entirely new painting ('Defacement – The Death Of Michael Stewart'). It becomes clear that* **Jean** *is making something now that is deeply personal and biographical.*

Andy   How do you know what to do? What goes where?

Jean *doesn't answer. He works as if in a trance now. Under the control of an urgent need to create this work . . .*

Andy *continues to film* **Jean** *at work. Here again the audience sees – projected large – exactly what* **Andy**'s *roving camera captures. If possible, all that* **Andy** *is filming – for he is a great artist in this medium – is also a work of art, and a valuable one.*

So begins a process, a dance . . .

Jean *painting . . .*

Andy *filming, moving . . .*

. . . and this is only interrupted when **Jean** *can't help but notice that he is being filmed.*

Jean *looks at the camera, then at* **Andy**, *then decides, against his better instincts, that maybe this moment is a collaboration also, and so lets it happen.*

Jean *resumes painting, as* **Andy** *moves the camera in and out.*

Andy   I've got a great idea. How about you take your shirt off. I film you painting without your shirt on.

Jean   Why?

Andy   It'd look so great. It'll make the film better.

Jean   You're playing with me.

Andy   Ah. No. But you can trust me. I've made a lot of movies now. It'll just be a so much better film . . . with your shirt off I think.

Jean *stares at* **Andy**. *They lock eyes on each other.*

Jean   Since when are we making a film?

Andy   Oh I've been making one . . . this whole time.

Jean *takes the camera off* **Andy**, *pointing it at him instead.*

Jean   I got a better idea. You take *your* shirt off. You know? How about that instead?

Andy   No, you don't wanna see that.

Jean   Maybe I do. That'd be great, right? Maybe *that'd* make a better film.

Andy   You really don't. I'm such a mess. Underneath. From what Valerie did.

Jean   You take yours off . . . and maybe I'll take mine off, that's the deal.

A stand off.

Andy   You'll take your shirt off? Okay. I guess I could . . .

So **Andy** *takes his shirt off, revealing a torso criss-crossed with surgical scars.*

Andy   But . . . I warned you.

Andy *stands before* **Jean** *with his shirt off and finally, defiantly, strikes a model's pose.*

Andy   There.

Jean (*touched by the sight of the scars*)   I'm sorry, man. She really messed you up.

Jean *turns the camera off and puts it aside.*

Andy *then goes to a full length mirror and films his reflection, and in close-up his scars.* (*We see, projected large, what the camera sees.*)

Andy   Behold! – The creature in the mirror. No wonder they call me a vampire. I try. I do try. I dye my own wigs. My eyebrows. It's no use. Why can't I be beautiful? You know? You'd think there would've been *a moment* . . . everybody else gets at least *a moment* . . .

Beat.

He's really tough on some people.

Jean   Who?

Andy   God.

Jean *pauses, looks at* **Andy***. He is moved by the sight of* **Andy***, who now has tears in his eyes.*

Andy   Lying on the operating table, a bullet, through my stomach, liver, oesophagus, and lungs, I heard the surgeon say 'He has no chance.' And only when the surgeon was told I was famous did the asshole decide to work hard and sew me up. If I ever go into a hospital again I won't come out, I know it. Next time they'll realise right away who I am and

I'll fall victim to the distracted medical attention all celebrities receive from over-awed staff. A little fame you survive a hospital, too much fame, you're dead.

Beat.

But the film's about you, Jean. It's about you, Jean. I really think this record of you could last forever. We never know what, of what we do, will survive.

Jean *finally takes off his shirt and resumes painting.*

Andy   Keep painting. Don't stop. I'll film you while you work.

Andy *picks up the camera and resumes filming* **Jean**.

Andy   Are you getting clean? Jean?

Jean   Why you say that?

Andy   Are you clean? Are you getting clean?

Jean   Three months, man. Three months, I'm good.

Andy   Because Jean, you have to live. And I get it, you've already convinced the market you're gonna die soon from doing so much heroin, and *nothing* pushes up prices like the promise of early death, nothing. But you don't have to do that, Jean. You can be great and live to see it.

Jean *paints*. **Andy** *films*.

Jean's *door phone buzzer sounds*, brrrrrrrr . . . brrrrrr . . . brrrrrr. *Several times.* **Jean** *doesn't react.*

Andy   This is even worse than Mick and Jerry's. I'd start to think about bodyguards, Jean. Crazy people are everywhere nowadays.

The buzzer goes again. **Andy** *grabs this first chance to put his shirt back on, as* **Jean** *goes to the window, opens it and calls down.*

Jean (*out window*)   Hey! Listen man, why don't you call before you come over!

Voice of Surprise Guest One (*off*)   Come on, man! We're hitting the park! Let's go, brother!

Jean   No!

Jean *slams the window then returns to the couch to smoke his joint.*

Jean   Everyone wants your blood.

Jean *returns to work on the small personal canvas.*

Andy *is now filming close-ups of the spilled cash.*

Andy   I love this.

Jean *puts down the red paint, and – using a stick of black pastel – starts to write an upside down question mark and then, at a distance, a second question mark, right way up.*

Jean *is writing 'DEFACEMENT' on the canvas now, between the question marks and ending with a copyright symbol.*

Andy   'Defacement.' With a copyright symbol and a question mark. Why?

Jean   I don't want to talk about it.

Andy   Why? Why not?

Jean   Because Michael is in the hospital, you know, in a coma.

Andy *keeps filming . . .*

Andy   Is 'defacement' what the cops charge you with when they catch you doing graffiti? Or is this about what they did to Michael's face?

Andy *keeps filming . . .*

What are you thinking?

Jean (*annoyed*)   Andy –

Andy   Right now?

Jean   Nothing.

Beat.

I put a lot down . . . and then I take a lot away . . . and until something tells me, tells me it's done and I should stop.

Andy But what determines what goes and what stays? (*Beat.*) Jean?

Jean Determines?

Beat.

I don't analyse it. It's sacred.

Andy Sacred?

Jean Yeah. You analyse it, you kill it off, you know. Can you stop with the filming now?

Jean *paints.*

Andy What are you thinking about now?

Jean Taking that camera out of your hands.

Andy Why?

Jean You're gonna ruin the painting.

Andy Maybe it will make the painting better?

Jean I doubt it. Maybe. But I doubt it.

Andy Two pieces of art at the same time –

Jean Don't think it works like that.

Andy – twice as powerful

Jean Just stop talking, man. I gotta finish this.

He paints quickly now, more violently, frustration clearly visible.

Andy Julian says your work is primal. What do you think of that?

Jean What? Like an ape?

Andy Well, let's –

Jean A primate? Like a primate?

Andy   You're Haitian Puerto Rican. You feel that that's in your art?

And then – the door phone buzzer goes again – brrrrrrr.

Andy   So your influences are –?

Jean *ignores this, until – brrrrrrrrrrrrrrrr brrrrrrrrrrrrrrr!*

Jean *finally goes to the window, opens it, calls down . . .*

Jean   GO AWAY!

Voice of Surprise Guest Two (*off*)   Hey, Jean! Let us up, man! Got some friends here wanna meet you! Let's hang out!

Jean   GO AWAY! NO!

Jean *grabs a bucket of water used for cleaning brushes, goes back to the window and throws it down on the unseen caller.*

Voice of Surprise Guest Two (*off*)   What the fuck, man?! Shit!

Jean   GO AWAY!

He slams the window again and goes back to the painting. **Andy** *keeps filming, pointing camera right at* **Jean** *. . .*

Andy   Your influences?

Jean (*sarcastic*)   Film.

Andy   So you think art should disturb?

Jean   Art should disturb the comfortable . . . comfort the disturbed.

Andy   Oh, I looove that. Can I steal it?

Jean   You're Andy Warhol.

Beat.

Come on, man, turn that off now, I'm serious.

Still **Andy** *films as –* **Jean**, *with his black pastel, draws in a central black silhouette between the two cops.*

Andy   You're attracted to violence?

Jean   No, man. Violence . . . is attracted to me.

Andy   Is that why your paintings are filled with so much death?

Jean   THEY'RE NOT! THEY'RE NOT! WHERE? WHERE? WHERE'S THE DEATH? YOU DON'T GET IT, MAN.

Andy   No, I don't get it!

Jean   WE'VE BEEN MAKING ALL THESE PAINTINGS TOGETHER AND YOU STILL DON'T GET IT.

Andy   Then what are they filled with? What?

Jean   I'M TRYING TO RAISE THE DEAD! YOU KNOW? I WANT TO BRING THE DEAD BACK TO LIFE! YOU WANT TO KNOW WHY I PAINT? THAT'S WHY. I'M PAINTING THIS, RIGHT NOW . . . FOR *MICHAEL*. IT'S NOT FOR PARAMOUNT, MAN. IT'S NOT FOR BRUNO OR SHAFRAZIS. IT'S NOT FOR SOME FUCKIN' *BUYER*. It's for Michael. It's for Michael in Bellevue. And if I . . .

Andy *says nothing, but keeps filming . . .*

Andy   'And if' . . . keep going . . .

Jean *is reluctant to say more.*

Andy   Jean! Explain!

Jean   Where I come from we don't talk about everything, we just do it. I'm not saying anything more. Words are your thing. I'm tired of playing by your rules, you know.

Andy   But you have to explain this. You're painting the beating of Michael. He's in Bellevue. And if you . . .

Jean   . . . if I paint it right . . . the right colours and the right symbols, images, the right magical properties . . . he'll recover. He'll wake up. No bruises. No cuts. Paintings can have supernatural power if you imbue them with them. These symbols, these images. Wherever they come from they have a power. They're like . . . *incantations*. It's a ritual, you know. Ancient ritual. Healing the sick, bringing the dead back to life. It's not all about having a brand, man. It can be about . . .

Andy   About?

Jean   . . . saving a life.

Andy   Oh my God, that's so great. It's like a whole Haitian thing. Like voodoo. *Art can save lives*. It's like a whole voodoo thing.

Jean *paints . . . as* **Andy** *films.*

Andy   My God, my work seems so shallow now. Yours is like a black mass? (*Pause*.) I think this film's gonna be so great for you, Jean. I think people are really gonna admire you when they see my film.

The sound of the door opens, and in walks . . . **Maya**.

Maya   Jean! You gotta come with me right now!

Jean   What?

Maya   The doctors couldn't stop the bleeding. He's gone. Michael's gone. The Stewarts have this family lawyer and they want us to come down to his office. And we need to bring all the photos you took. It's important evidence if we're gonna put these fuckers in prison. Okay? We gotta go.

Jean *shakes his head.*

Maya   What? Jean, Jean let's go.

Jean   I can't.

Maya   What do you mean?

Jean I can't go there.

Maya We have to go there, *right now*! Their lawyer is waiting for us.

Beat.

It's *Michael*. They killed Michael.

Jean I can't! . . . right now.

Maya Why? Why not?

Andy *is still surreptitiously filming . . .*

Jean Because, *because* . . . you don't understand, that could have been me, what happened to Michael . . . and if we cause trouble . . .

Maya WHAT?

Jean . . . *they'll come for me*. They will.

Maya What are you even talking about?

Jean You don't know, you don't know what it's like to be on this side of things. You don't understand. Do you want this to happen to me? Do you? Want to see me dead? Want to see me dead too?

Jean *looks at* **Andy**.

Andy I need to make a call.

Andy *exits*.

Maya Jean, you have to come with me. Yes or no? I have to go down there, I need you to come with me. Just yes or no, Jean?

Jean *doesn't move.* **Maya** *breaks into tears.*

Maya God!

Maya *starts to go and then comes back.*

The pictures. The Polaroids. Gimme the pictures. I need the pictures.

Jean *gives her the photos. She looks at them.*

Maya   Did you even look at these? Shit.

Maya *exits in tears.*

Alone, **Jean** *manifests his fear and shock and guilt and horror and anger and rage. He starts to shake. In a daze, he walks across the room, not knowing what to do with himself. Grief breaks over him. It's too much.*

In distress, he goes to the tape desk and hits play. More 'Turnaroundphrase – Live at the Newport Jazz Festival, Berlin'.

He then goes to the coffee table, reaches underneath it . . . and takes out a box.

From the box he takes out . . . a syringe and some heroin, and a spoon and a lighter . . . which he lays out on the coffee table to prepare his fix. He pauses when his eye fixes on **Andy**'s *film camera . . .*

He looks at the camera, then opens the body of the camera and starts to pull out the film, faster and faster, destroying **Andy**'s *film. He then goes to* **Andy**'s *camera bag and takes out cans of Super 16 footage shot earlier, exposing the undeveloped film, unravelling the film. The music ends.*

Enter **Andy**.

Andy   Pat's coming over to get me. I thought we should –

Only now does **Andy** *see what* **Jean** *is doing.*

Andy   Jean. STOP! What are you doing? Stop! No, you can't do that! That's my film! STOP THAT! That's a masterpiece! It's priceless!

Jean   You ruined it. You ruined the painting. You spoiled it, killed its magic.

Andy   What are you talking about? Are you crazy? YOU DESTROYED MY WORK! WHAT HAVE YOU –?

Jean   YOU DESTROYED MINE! I was trying to bring Michael round. I could'a saved him. I was trying to save him. But you ruined it, Andy. Now he's gone.

Andy   WHAT HAVE YOU DONE? You're a real terrorist, Jean.

Jean   And it's your fault, man. You messed it up. By filming! Filming, you stole the spirit from the painting by doing that. You killed it. Took all its power away. Understand? And now, now Michael's dead. Because you filmed your fucking film, man!

Andy   I was just making . . .

Jean   No wonder you drive everyone crazy. You know. Because you won't stop filming. And you tell *me* I have to live? Huh? Shit. Damn. You want *me* to live? WHAT ABOUT *YOU*, ANDY?! You gotta have a camera everywhere you go? Man, you're so afraid to live you put a camera and a tape recorder between you and everything else. What the hell?

Andy   I make art. I'm an artist. That's all I am.

Jean   No, man. You make *death*. You're not living.

Andy   Oh my God, you can't say things like this. These are terrible things to say to a person. I make beautiful things. Carefully. Very carefully. I produce, out of what I see.

Jean   'Produce'? You *re*-produce. You're the champ Andy, the King of repetition, of structure, of order . . . the champ of 'pretty', boom . . . the champ of 'famous', boom . . . the champ of the invisible, of surfaces, boom for real.

Andy   You have a real mean streak in you, Jean.

Jean   What about . . . what about mysteries, man . . . dreams, you know . . . pain, shit, blood, magic, the divine? What about miracles? (*Pause.*) You drink blood –

Andy   Oh God!

Jean   – young people's blood. We're both addicts, Andy. Were both 'users'.

Andy   Stop this, Jean. What's come over you?

Jean *then picks up the film camera and points it at* **Andy**.

Jean   I wanna make a film about you now. I'm filming you now. How 'bout I ask you questions? You know? Why you working with me Andy?

Andy   There's no film in there!

Jean   Why you working with me? Huh? Why's Andy Warhol working with me?!

Andy *has had enough. He snaps.*

Andy   BECAUSE BRUNO ASKED ME TO!

Jean   No, why are you really working with me? The truth!

Andy   BECAUSE BRUNO BEGGED ME TO! And you're young. And interesting. And I *prefer* young people, because they're usually less likely to talk about the subject that least interests me: death.

Jean   That's not a reason. Tell the truth. You wanna be cool again, steal my identity.

Andy   This is art, identity has no place.

Jean   You can't tell a black man that. Won't work, Andy. You know what you get when you mix *ivory black* (*Jean*) and *titanium white* (*Andy*)?

Andy   Wait, I know this one . . . Grey?

Jean   Your first right answer. You can't be me. Not ever.

Andy   I *can't*? What devastating news! Gee! And I was *soo* looking forward to fucking Madonna . . .

Jean I'm gonna ask you again . . . why are you working with me? Why? WHY –

Andy SO I COULD HAVE JEAN-MICHEL BASQUIAT IN MY FILM! THAT'S WHY. I WAS HERE TO MAKE A FILM UNTIL YOU RUINED IT.

Jean *is stunned by this, mystified.*

Jean *Film*? That was *it*? You don't care . . . about our paintings?

Andy As much as someone who doesn't paint anymore can care about painting. You won. The boxing match. 'World's greatest painter', attaboy. But why are you working with *me*? Jean? That's even more mysterious.

Jean No. Uh uh. I'm asking the questions. Why did you give up painting? When I first handed you a brush on day one, you looked scared.

Andy *rises to go.*

Jean Stay there. Stay there, Andy. It's my movie now.

Andy This is getting super ugly. Stop this.

Jean *aims the camera at* **Andy** *like a gun.*

Jean *I'm* filming *you*. Answer. Answer the question. You said you stopped believing in painting. No great painter has ever given up painting. But you stopped. How come?

Andy You're a total gangster. A Puerto Rican hood, like a scorpion, trying to scare someone into giving you everything they have in their pockets. Jean, you *have* to be more civilised.

Jean Don't say that to me, Andy. Don't look down on me or we can't see each other. Ever again. We're equal. Or we're nothing. Never look down on me. Answer the question.

Andy I'm just saying it's no wonder security guards follow you in an expensive store. They think you're going to do something. Not because you're black. Not because you're black. But because you have this look in your eye. People can all see that look in your eye.

Jean   Man. No wonder they all committed suicide. Or else tried to shoot you. Why did you give up painting? WHY?

Andy   Because . . .

Jean   The truth, man! WHY'D YOU GIVE UP?

Andy *finally erupts.*

Andy   BECAUSE ANDREW WARHOLA FROM PITTSBURGH PAINTS! *HE* PAINTS! ANDY WARHOL, OF NEW YORK CITY, DOESN'T.

Beat.

Andy Warhol . . . only takes photographs . . . makes prints . . . makes films . . . and goes to parties and feeds pigeons in the fucken park!

Jean   Why?

Andy   It's safer.

Jean   Why's it safer?

Andy   It works better . . . at *distracting* –

Jean   From what?

Andy   . . . a lifelong loathing of himself.

Jean   You loathe yourself?

Andy   LOOK AT ME! LOOK AT ME, JEAN!

Beat.

It's not so uncommon. My whole mangled childhood – even when I first came to New York – I painted, created beautiful things. Painting helped, distracted me, gave my eyes *something* beautiful to look at. But it stopped working after a while. Painting became painful . . . drop the letter T from paint, that's what it became for me. So, *printing* . . . from then on . . . that was better . . . screen-printing, photography, brands, mass reproduction, films. A change of medication. So there it is. Ondrej Warhola, the despised little runt from steel town America, with all his self-hatred, he *had* to paint. I. Stopped. Andy Warhol lives with the consequences.

Beat.

Oh, and for the record, Jean, you offering me that paint-brush on the first day? That was as scary as Valerie pointing her gun at my heart.

Beat.

Are we finished, Mr DeMille? (*Holds out his hand.*) Camera?

*But **Jean** doesn't pass the camera over. He goes to the window and throws the camera out the window, into the street. Smash.*

Jean   You ruined my painting. You killed my friend.

Andy *is sucker-punched by this.*

You don't really believe I killed Michael, do you?

Jean   Yeah. You kill everyone.

Andy   My God don't say that, Jean! (*Falls to his knees, makes the sign of the cross.*) I'm praying, that you're wrong. Words last forever you know. You can't say things like that to someone, don't you know that? Did no one teach you? Then you need to learn it, Jean. You really have terrible manners.

Jean   I'm not gonna let you exploit me anymore, Andy. Okay?

Andy   Here we go again!

Jean   I'm sick of everyone exploiting me, you know. It's over.

Andy   Why do people accuse me of exploiting them? 'Andy is playing with people's lives again!' 'Andy is evil!' 'A vampire

living on young blood!' Like I have all this *power* over
people.

Jean   You do. That's coz you do.

Andy   NO! I DON'T! It's just the opposite!

Andy *grows emotional, even tearful, as he gathers up all the pulled
film stock, and admits to his secret life . . .*

Jean   You just don't realize it.

Andy   When I was young I discovered that it was safer just
to watch . . . and so I watched, and I became a mirror, and I
learned to say 'Oh gee' and 'Gosh' and 'That's so great' and
the more I encouraged people, the more outrageously they
performed for me. So, when Freddie Herko ran across my
studio, right through the window and fell three storeys to
the street below, yes, I said 'Gee, I wish I'd filmed it, that
would've made a great movie'. Shoot me, I didn't push him.

Andy *gathers up his things, prepares to go . . .*

So now I'm supposed to be this, what? This leader of some
sexual carnival? But the truth about me, Jean – if you
actually want the truth about me – is that I've been to one
orgy in my life and I was asked to leave because all I did was
observe. I started one real love affair in my life, one, back in
the 1950s . . . with my television set. And then in 1964 I
married my tape recorder, the acquisition of which ended
whatever emotional life I might have had – but I was glad to
see it go. And so now my average day is all about work until
eight at night when I go to Serendipity and eat exactly three
bites of hot-fudge sundae, and then I stand around getting
photographed with celebrities that wanna stand around
getting photographed with me. Mother, before she died,
used to keep the light on, waiting for me to come home in
the early hours. Now I keep it on for myself. Turn it on
when I go out. I see it from the street when I get home, and
I think 'That's nice, someone waited up'. And for all this, for

all this . . . they call me evil. (*Puts on dark glasses.*) The Prince of Darkness.

Andy, *now ready to leave – his wig checked in the mirror and his calm persona at last restored – stops to evaluate the incomplete Paramount picture . . .*

Andy   I think we're done. Don't you? Let's just say we are. That's the great thing about contemporary art – who can fucken tell?

Andy *exits. The door slams.* **Jean** *only now realises* **Andy** *is gone.*

Jean, *alone, returns to the couch and prepares the heroin to shoot up . . . holds a lighter under a spoon, cooking up the dope, prepares to fill the syringe, etc. . . . .*

Andy *quietly re-enters unseen . . . watches all this . . . forcing himself to watch.*

Jean *looks at* **Andy**, *then starts to fill the syringe with heroin . . .*

Jean   You're not gonna tell me to stop?

Andy   Honey, you're not my first junkie.

Jean   I'm not a junkie. I'm gonna clean up. Go clean.

Andy   When people are ready to, they change. They never do it before then, and sometimes they die before they get around to it. I hope you don't die, Jean, before you get around to it.

Andy *takes some brushes and a new, blank canvas and lays it on the floor.*

Jean   I'm gonna live. You know? I'm gonna be immortal. Immortal, man.

He cries.

Andy, I'm hurting! I'm hurting!

Andy, *downstage, kneeling in front of the canvas . . . slowly offers a paintbrush to* **Jean**, *without turning.*

Andy   Since I was shot, everything is such a dream to me. Like I don't know whether I'm alive or whether I died already. I wasn't afraid before. And having been dead once, I shouldn't feel fear. But I am afraid. Not of death, *of life*. You were right about me. Living is the tough part.

Jean   You're not afraid of death?

Andy   Death is like going to Bloomingdale's, it's nothing.

Jean *rises, goes to* **Andy**, *sees what he's doing, then takes the brush and joins* **Andy** *on the floor. Both paint, side by side.*

Andy *is painting with a bigger brush than usual.* **Jean** *notices.*

Jean   It's messy.

Andy   Yeah well. What are ya gonna do?

Jean   The next time you die, Andy, I'll bring you back to life. I know I can do it.

Andy   I wanna see *that* painting. What'll be in it?

Jean   Soup tins . . . hearts . . . scars . . . some other crazy shit . . . a crucifix . . . and wigs . . . lots of like flying wigs . . . wigs with wings . . . love.

Andy   But Jean you've already brought me back to life, which is super great because God's had it his own way for far too long.

They look into each other's eyes.

Andy   Jean-Michel Basquiat . . . I order you to live forever . . . forever and ever. And with all that extra time you simply *have* to learn how to use a vacuum cleaner.

Jean (*laughing*)   I love you Andy.

Andy   Oh shuttup and paint. Just paint. Or we'll never be finished.

Curtain.

Acknowledgements

The Andy Warhol Foundation

Andrew Wylie Agency

Methuen Drama Modern Plays

include

Bola Agbaje
Edward Albee
Ayad Akhtar
Jean Anouilh
John Arden
Peter Barnes
Sebastian Barry
Clare Barron
Alistair Beaton
Brendan Behan
Edward Bond
William Boyd
Bertolt Brecht
Howard Brenton
Amelia Bullmore
Anthony Burgess
Leo Butler
Jim Cartwright
Lolita Chakrabarti
Caryl Churchill
Lucinda Coxon
Tim Crouch
Shelagh Delaney
Ishy Din
Claire Dowie
David Edgar
David Eldridge
Dario Fo
Michael Frayn
John Godber
James Graham
David Greig
John Guare
Lauren Gunderson
Peter Handke
David Harrower
Jonathan Harvey
Robert Holman
David Ireland
Sarah Kane

Barrie Keeffe
Jasmine Lee-Jones
Anders Lustgarten
Duncan Macmillan
David Mamet
Patrick Marber
Martin McDonagh
Arthur Miller
Alistair McDowall
Tom Murphy
Phyllis Nagy
Anthony Neilson
Peter Nichols
Ben Okri
Joe Orton
Vinay Patel
Joe Penhall
Luigi Pirandello
Stephen Poliakoff
Lucy Prebble
Peter Quilter
Mark Ravenhill
Philip Ridley
Willy Russell
Jackie Sibblies Drury
Sam Shepard
Martin Sherman
Chris Shinn
Wole Soyinka
Simon Stephens
Kae Tempest
Anne Washburn
Laura Wade
Theatre Workshop
Timberlake Wertenbaker
Roy Williams
Snoo Wilson
Frances Ya-Chu Cowhig
Benjamin Zephaniah

Methuen Drama Contemporary Dramatists

include

John Arden (two volumes)
Arden & D'Arcy
Peter Barnes (three volumes)
Sebastian Barry
Mike Bartlett
Clare Barron
Brad Birch
Dermot Bolger
Edward Bond (ten volumes)
Howard Brenton (two volumes)
Leo Butler (two volumes)
Richard Cameron
Jim Cartwright
Caryl Churchill (two volumes)
Complicite
Sarah Daniels (two volumes)
Nick Darke
David Edgar (three volumes)
David Eldridge (two volumes)
Ben Elton
Per Olov Enquist
Dario Fo (two volumes)
Michael Frayn (four volumes)
John Godber (four volumes)
Paul Godfrey
James Graham (two volumes)
David Greig
John Guare
Lee Hall (two volumes)
Katori Hall
Peter Handke
Jonathan Harvey (two volumes)
Iain Heggie
Israel Horovitz
Declan Hughes
Terry Johnson (three volumes)
Sarah Kane
Barrie Keeffe
Bernard-Marie Koltès (two volumes)
Franz Xaver Kroetz
Kwame Kwei-Armah
David Lan
Bryony Lavery
Deborah Levy
Doug Lucie

Alistair MacDowall
Sabrina Mahfouz
David Mamet (six volumes)
Patrick Marber
Martin McDonagh
Duncan McLean
David Mercer (two volumes)
Anthony Minghella (two volumes)
Rory Mullarkey
Tom Murphy (six volumes)
Phyllis Nagy
Anthony Neilson (three volumes)
Peter Nichol (two volumes)
Philip Osment
Gary Owen
Louise Page
Stewart Parker (two volumes)
Joe Penhall (two volumes)
Stephen Poliakoff (three volumes)
David Rabe (two volumes)
Mark Ravenhill (three volumes)
Christina Reid
Philip Ridley (two volumes)
Willy Russell
Eric-Emmanuel Schmitt
Ntozake Shange
Sam Shepard (two volumes)
Martin Sherman (two volumes)
Christopher Shinn (two volumes)
Joshua Sobel
Wole Soyinka (two volumes)
Simon Stephens (five volumes)
Shelagh Stephenson
David Storey (three volumes)
C. P. Taylor
Sue Townsend
Judy Upton (two volumes)
Michel Vinaver (two volumes)
Arnold Wesker (two volumes)
Peter Whelan
Michael Wilcox
Roy Williams (four volumes)
David Williamson
Snoo Wilson (two volumes)
David Wood (two volumes)
Victoria Wood

For a complete listing of
Methuen Drama titles, visit:
www.bloomsbury.com/drama

Follow us on Twitter and keep up to date
with our news and publications
@MethuenDrama